So You're
70!

Mike Haskins & Clive Whichelow

summersdale

SO YOU'RE 70!

Summersdale Publishers Ltd
46 West Street
Chichester
West Sussex
PO19 1RP
UK

www.summersdale.com

Printed and bound in China

ISBN 13: 978-1-84024-646-9

INTRODUCTION

Oh dear, 70! At 50 you could kid yourself you were still quite young; and compared to 70 you were! Even at 60 you weren't quite retired, but 70 – that's pretty old! You're older than Israel, Sri Lanka and Biffo the Bear.

You're now even too old to look forward to a bus pass, and you'll never swim with dolphins – unless one finds its way into your walk-in bath.

But at least you're someone the rest of the family looks up to – especially when they want to borrow some money.

And if you wake up from an afternoon nap sweating from a nightmare about being surrounded by multiple Grim Reapers, don't worry, it's just your lovely little grandchildren in their hoodies demanding yet another handout.

But it's not all bad news, you're still younger than Mrs Thatcher, Superman, and the speaking clock!

So, you're 70 – so what!

THE BASIC MYTHS ABOUT TURNING 70

You don't know what's fashionable any more – yes you do! You just keep listening to the same music, wearing the same clothes and keep your house decorated the same way – it all comes back into fashion every few years!

You're into your second childhood – not unless you count sleeping in the day and needing the toilet in the middle of the night.

You're past it! – well, at least that means you know where it is and can go back and find it again whenever you choose!

You're a grumpy old git – really? No work, free travel, people giving you their seat on crowded buses… what's to be grumpy about?

THINGS YOU WILL
NEVER NOW DO

Win Wimbledon (Even the 'veterans' are under 60 for goodness sake!).

Get a job as Tom Cruise or Angelina Jolie's stunt double.

The splits (except perhaps by accident – possibly while auditioning to be Tom Cruise or Angelina Jolie's stunt double).

YOUR LIFE WILL NOW CONSIST OF...

Feeding the entire bird population
of your neighbourhood.

Trying to find your glasses (try top
of head or dangling from
string round neck).

Attending exercise classes in an attempt
to regain the physique you had as
a lithe young 60-year-old.

DRESS CODE FOR THE OVER-70S – SOME DO'S AND DON'TS

Do avoid anything 'figure hugging' unless you're reasonably confident other people will want to hug your figure.

Don't think because you're at home all day you don't have to make an effort.

Do try to retain some dignity. Miniskirts and high heels just won't look right – especially on you men.

CULTURE CONVERTER

When speaking with people younger
than yourself it's no use talking about
things that happened before they were
born, they won't have a clue what you're
on about. So here is a handy culture
converter to translate your cultural
reference points to their equivalent.

CATEGORY	70s	MIDDLE AGED	YOUNG ADULTS	KIDS
Dominant cultural influence when growing up	World War Two	Swinging London	Rave scene	*Balamory*
Unpleasant experience during childhood	Being bombed	IRA campaign	Al Qaeda attacks	Watching *The X Factor*
Likely cause of youthful mind-blowing experience	Disney's *Fantasia*	LSD	Ecstasy	A day at Alton Towers
Fondly remembered early Christmas present	A satsuma	Action Man	Furbie	The entire contents of the Argos catalogue toy section
Point at which understanding of technology ceased	Sandwich toaster	Video recorder	Computer	Video iPod, particle accelerator, etc.
Exotic luxury	Bananas	Chop suey	Falafel	Chicken nuggets

HOW TO APPEAR YOUNGER THAN YOU ACTUALLY ARE

If you can't afford Botox, Polyfilla makes a cheap and cheerful substitute for filling in those wrinkles.

If bits of your body are beginning to sag, hang upside down while having your photograph taken, then invert the resulting picture when you display it.

Join a religious order which requires covering up your face, body, and grey hair.

GIVEAWAYS THAT WILL TELL PEOPLE YOU ARE OVER 70

Referring to people in their 60s as 'whippersnappers'.

Referring to the radio as 'the wireless'.

Beginning any threats you make with the words, 'If I was any younger I'd…'

THE MAIN EVENTS IN YOUR LIFE YOU CAN NOW LOOK FORWARD TO

Being three-quarters of a century old.

Becoming a great-grandparent – at last you're great at something!

Your second adolescence (presuming you're now growing out of your second childhood that is).

Being invited into local schools to tell the children what it was like during the war.

THE MAIN EVENTS IN YOUR LIFE IT'S LESS EASY TO LOOK FORWARD TO

Unexpectedly finding you need your neighbours to help you out of the bath.

Going out, then forgetting where you live.

Realising you no longer care if products have a 25-year guarantee.

CONVERSING WITH YOUNG PEOPLE (PART 1)

What you say and what they hear

'I beg your pardon?' = 'Please speak directly into my face as loud as you can while generally treating me like a complete idiot.'

'That reminds me...' = 'Let me once again tell you the entire history of my life in extraordinary detail.'

'I may be old but I'm not daft.' =
'There's nothing in my pockets
worth pinching.'

'So who's top of the pops then?' =
'I was around when Edison
invented the phonograph.'

STATISTICALLY SPEAKING

Seventy years may seem a long time but
you can sound younger by telling people
your age in months, days
or even hours e.g.:

'Of course I'm a youngster really. Only
840 months old, you know.'

'I am a mere 25,567 days old.'

'Old! I'm not old! I've only been here for 613,607 hours. And I was asleep or on the toilet for a lot of those!'

Unfortunately, in terms of seconds you're into the billions (2,208,984,840).

Perhaps it's best to go back to calling it 70 years!

Just think, if you'd set off at a pace of three miles per hour the moment you were born (OK, you'd have to do the first bit in your pram) you would so far have travelled 1,840,821 miles.

That means that by now you could have walked round the earth almost 74 times!

Or you could have gone to the moon and back at least 3.5 times.

Then you'd have an excuse for feeling so tired!

NOW YOU'RE 70 THE FOLLOWING WILL BE YOUR NATURAL ENEMIES

Cheats who've had Botox, eye-lifts, and hair transplants.

People whose hair hasn't yet turned grey and/or people with hair.

Distances of more than ten yards that have to be covered without anything to hold on to.

A LIST OF CONTROVERSIAL OPINIONS YOU WILL NOW BE EXPECTED TO HOLD

'"Illegal immigrant" means anyone who arrived in this country after the Angles and Saxons.'

'Birching's too good for them.'

'Pensioners should be allowed to carry guns for self-protection.'

'Groups of youths found hanging around after dark should be collected by the military and used for target practice.'

CONVERSING WITH YOUNG PEOPLE (PART 2)

What they say and what you hear

'Tell us your memories from the war.' =
'I have discovered evidence that you
were once a Nazi collaborator.'

'Would you like my bus seat?' =
'Sit down before you fall down
you poor old sod.'

'I bet you've seen a few changes in your time.' = 'So what *were* horse-drawn buses and rickets like?'

'Do you want any help packing your shopping?' = 'You'll do yourself a mischief trying to lift that large jar of Marmite.'

THINGS YOU CAN NOW GET AWAY WITH THAT YOU COULDN'T PREVIOUSLY

Using your false teeth to crimp a pie crust.

Becoming a highly active sex maniac.

Suddenly going deaf when approached
by charity collectors.

Getting neighbours to do your shopping
and gardening for you.

Making sexist and racist comments
because you 'don't understand
the modern world'.

THINGS YOU ARE NOW LIKELY TO HAVE IN YOUR HOME

A garden security light which can be set off by the fluttering of a moth's wings.

A small dog that the rest of your family dislike intensely.

A stairlift (doesn't matter whether you need one or not – they're fun!).

THINGS THAT YOU WILL TAKE A SUDDEN INTEREST IN

Any new tablets that a friend has just been prescribed by the doctor.

The Budget – hoping your pension will be miraculously trebled.

The obituaries column – just to see who you've outlived today.

Places where you can keep warm without it costing you a penny.

HOORAY! THINGS YOU'LL NEVER HAVE TO DO AGAIN

Work!

Consider what clothes might be in fashion.

Feel that you're wasting the doctor's time.

Bring up any more children.

BOO! THINGS YOU WON'T BE DOING AGAIN

Being hired on the basis of your looks rather than your ability.

Running to catch the bus.

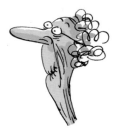

Having candles on your birthday cake
correctly matching your age.

SHATTERING MOMENTS TO COME SOON

You drop off mid-conversation when talking to yourself.

You have to check whether there's a 'comfort stop' before embarking on journeys over half an hour long.

You refuse your favourite food because it's 'a bit hard to chew'.

You discover that the rest of the bowls
team are younger than you.

You realise the bath isn't filling up
because you've forgotten to
close the door on the side.

PRODUCTS ONLY THE OVER-70S WILL REMEMBER

Sweets sold in the form of 'junior smoker's' kits.

78 rpm records.
(What's an rpm? What's a record?)

Powdered egg.

BEING 70 IS...

... being a bit long in the tooth – it should be a bit long in the teeth, but that's ageing for you.

... meeting someone at bingo rather than meeting someone and – bingo!

... when short pants are your summer breathing pattern rather than your summer wardrobe.

... looking at a life within your means rather than a meaning in your life.

... being as old as the hills but having a bit of difficulty walking over them.

THINGS YOU SHOULD NOT HAVE IN YOUR HOME

Underwear from your youth still in regular service.

Any of those 'change your life' books
– let's face it, you're not going
to start now.

Go-faster stripes on the side of your
Zimmer frame.

AARRGH! THINGS YOU NEVER THOUGHT WOULD HAPPEN

You start planning your day round your favourite TV programmes.

You consider getting a little part-time job to stave off the boredom.

You boast about having all your own
teeth (or even worse, just some
of your own teeth).

You've stopped looking like your
parents and started to look
like your grandparents.

YOUR NEW OUTLOOK ON LIFE

You're as old as you feel – unfortunately, some days you feel about 98.

It's too late to give up drinking or smoking now.

You may be 70 on the outside but you're only 20 on the inside – unfortunately it's your outside that has to carry your inside round everywhere.

You've seen it all before – although admittedly last time you saw it, it was in slightly sharper focus.

YOUR NEW WEEKLY HIGHLIGHTS

Having a nice Sunday morning drive
when all those young idiots
are still in bed.

Spending the whole weekend doing
the giant crossword.

Your regular appointment to have your feet done at the NHS's expense.

Despite having all week to do your shopping, saving it all till Saturday morning so you can drive the people who have to work all week crazy!

THINGS YOU WILL DESPERATELY TRY TO AVOID

Becoming a moaning old git.

Relatives who have taken a sudden
interest in the contents of your will.

Watching the TV with the volume turned up to maximum.

THINGS YOU SHOULD NOT HAVE IN YOUR CAR

A volume booster for your satnav.

A road map showing all the public toilets marked with an X.

A tartan rug over your legs to keep you warm while you're driving.

A red flag for your spouse to walk in front of the vehicle waving.

THINGS YOU WON'T BE DOING ON HOLIDAY ANY MORE

Playing beach volleyball.

Waking up in the morning fuzzy-headed and not remembering where the hell you are (though on second thoughts...)

Dancing till dawn to your favourite music – Connie Francis and Perry Como are probably not on the local nightclub's playlist any more.

YOUTH-ENHANCERS TO AVOID

Anti-wrinkle cream – if it really works it might cause you to disappear completely.

Liposuction – don't try having all your fat removed, it could be all that's holding you together.

Hair extensions – they don't
do them in grey or white.

HOW TO BE PHILOSOPHICAL
ABOUT BEING 70

Antiques are always more valuable than any more recently produced equivalents.

If you've still got your marbles you can still play the game.

It's not 70. It's 55 plus VAT.

REASONS TO BE CHEERFUL

You're still younger than Clint Eastwood,
Joan Collins, Sophia Loren, Brigitte
Bardot and Sean Connery.

If your laughter lines are anything
to go by you've had a fabulous
fun-filled life. Seventy not out!

Your teeth are looking in better shape than ever before – so what if they spend all night in a glass next to your bed.

www.summersdale.com